Law of Attraction

Manifestation Exercises

Transform All Areas of Your Life with Tested LOA & Quantum Physics Secrets

By Elena G.Rivers

Copyright Elena G.Rivers © 2017, 2019

www.LOAforSuccess.com

do not participate in or encourage electronic piracy of copyrighted materials.

Legal Notice:

This book is copyright protected. It for personal use on

Disclaimer Notice:

Please note the information contained in this document is for educational and entertainment purposes only. Every attempt has been made to provide accurate, up to date and completely reliable information. No warranties of any kind are expressed or implied.

Readers acknowledge that the author is not engaging in the rendering of legal, financial, medical or professional advice. By reading this document, the reader agrees that under no circumstances are we responsible for any losses, direct or indirect, which are incurred as a result of the use of information contained within this document, including, but not limited to, errors, omissions, or inaccuracies.

ISBN-10: 1544020228
ISBN-13: 978-1544020228

Table of Contents

You create your own universe as you go along.

– Winston Churchill

Introduction

The Law of Attraction has been highly publicized and has become the topic of books, CDs, and seminars. *The Secret*, a 2006 best seller, brought the Law of Attraction to the forefront for millions of people. Many have tried to put the Law of Attraction into practice only to end up with mixed results or disappointment. The most fundamental reason for this is that most discussions about the Law of Attraction approach it from a perspective that is <u>limited by our belief system</u>.

When I think of my childhood, I remember an old poster that I had on the wall of my room. The poster showed a seagull gracefully soaring against a vast blue sky with the words, "They can because they think they can." For every person who has not been able to manifest as they hoped, these words echo the reason why.

As long as we try to manifest from the mindset of the average person, we will not be able to experience our potential for manifesting. The reason is that conscious manifesting requires shifting from the common mindset to one that is conducive to manifesting. The problem is not that manifesting is difficult. The problem is that most of us lack control of our manifesting abilities. Unless we learn to take charge of the manifesting process, we will be like a person who gets behind the wheel of a car who has never learned to drive.

I need to clarify a statement that I just made. Learning to manifest consciously is less about taking "charge" as it is learning to allow and accept our current experience of life. Perhaps a more accurate way to describe manifesting is to compare it to trying to remember someone's name. We try to remember the person's name without success. When we stop trying to remember the name, the name comes to us. Manifesting works the same way. The universe, or consciousness, does not make an effort to manifest. Manifesting occurs effortlessly.

At every moment of our lives, new manifestations are appearing before us, manifestations that we attracted. We just have to contemplate our bodies to recognize this. At every moment, new cells are replacing old cells, and complex physiological processes are occurring. Each of these new cells or physiological processes is the result of a new potential manifesting itself.

To become conscious manifesters, we need to do the same thing that we would do anytime we want to learn a new skill, which is to look for someone who is already doing it and model them. By learning to model the qualities of the universe, we can become conscious manifesters. This book explores the characteristics of consciousness (I use *universe* and *consciousness* interchangeably throughout this book) and how to adopt these characteristics in our lives.

Adopting the characteristics for manifesting is the secondary reason behind why this book was written. My ultimate hope is that by embracing these qualities, you will discover <u>the truth of who you are</u>, which is more profound than anything you could ever manifest.

This book is designed to be a practical, step-by-step guide.

There are exercises waiting for you with each step.

My intention is to help you transform on a deeper level and enjoy the process.

If you happen to have any questions or simply wish to say hi, don't hesitate to email me.

In order to email me, be sure to join my newsletter:

www.loaforsuccess.com/newsletter

Then, reply to the first email I send you and let me know if you have any questions.

Please note, this is my personal email and it's not handled by my assistant.

That is why it's really the best way to keep in touch with me and share your experiences.

Now, back to the book- I highly recommend that you focus on just a few of your favorite exercises. you believe are the most important for you.

How will you know?

Ask yourself – when thinking about *the new me* with this new mindset, do I feel lighter and more excited? Would that help me change my life and manifest faster?

If the answer is *yes*, focus more on those.

Now- time to take some meaningful action here to help you transform!

Let's do this!

Thank you for taking an interest in this book. I truly believe it has the power to change your life.

Before we dive into the exercises, be sure to read through the next page as I have a free newsletter & surprise gift that I am offering. When combined with the teachings shared in this book, you will be given the advantage that will make everyone around you wonder what it is that you are doing.

Oh and this book is also available in audio format.

It could be handy to help you consolidate what you have learned and feed more mind with positive information while you're driving, working out or just chilling out.

You will find the audio edition of this book on our website:

www.LOAforSuccess.com/audiobooks

See you on the next page.

A Special Offer from Elena to Help You Manifest Faster.

The best way to get in touch with me is by joining my free email newsletter.

You can easily do it in a few seconds by visiting our private website at:

www.LOAforSuccess.com/newsletter

The best part?

When you sign up, you will instantly receive a free copy of an exclusive **LOA Workbook** that will help you raise your vibration in 5 days or less:

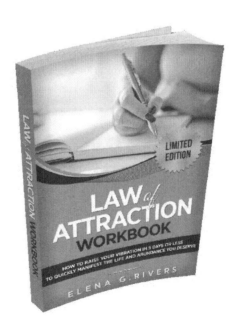

You will also be the first one to learn about my new releases, bonuses and other valuable resources to help you on your journey.

Sign up now and I'll "see you" in the first email.

No worries, I hate spam as much as you do.

I only send out valuable information and relevant resources😊

Love,

Elena

I attract to my life whatever I give my attention, energy, and focus to, whether positive or negative.

– Michael Losier

Chapter 1: The Truth about Manifesting

The truth about manifesting is that we have been doing it every moment of our lives; we are just unaware of it. It is the lack of this awareness that leads us to believe that manifesting does not work for us, or that it works with limited results.

Anytime that we dream at night, we experience ourselves as a projection of our sleeping self. The projected self, the dream self, experiences and engages with its dream world. Just as in our waking life where we believe we are a separate entities inhabiting the "real world," our dream self believes that it's separate in its dream world.

It is only when awaken that we realize that which we experienced during the night was just a dream. What we often do not take time to contemplate is that our sleeping self-manifested both our dream self and its dream world. Unlike our waking experience, our sleeping self-manifested our dream experience without any effort.

Both our dream experience and our "real world" experience are projections of consciousness.

We can think of the manifestation process like an old movie or a slide projector. Unlike the modern day projectors that are digitized, older movie projectors worked by projecting a beam of light through a film strip or slide, as in the slide projector. The image from the film strip or slide is then projected on to a screen. Similarly, we project consciousness, or awareness, on thought.

Thought is like an individual frame of a film strip or slide. It is projected by the light of consciousness onto to the screen of our minds, resulting in what we refer to as "experience." In this case, the screen is also consciousness. In fact, the thought, projection of thought, resulting experience, and the screen itself are all aspects of consciousness.

Going back to the movie projector metaphor, the image that appears on the screen and the screen itself are inseparable, just as the image and the projected light are inseparable from each other. The challenge that we have in manifesting is that we believe that we are separate from that which we want to manifest. Just as the light beam is inseparable from the image, we are inseparable from that which we want to manifest. It is this sense of separateness that creates our sense of difficulty in manifesting.

If you can entertain the parallel between the manifestation process and the dream world, here is a metaphor for the truth of who you are, and that metaphor is deep sleep. Deep sleep is like a slide projector without a slide. The beam of light travels into empty space without any slide to project. Deep sleep is like the movie projector without a film strip. The only thing that is being projected is the light itself.

During deep sleep, you have no sense of separation since there is nothing to experience, and you lose all sense of yourself. For this reason, deep sleep is a metaphor for pure consciousness.

All manifestation arises from consciousness. Without consciousness, no manifestation could exist. You are the projection of pure consciousness. Your experience of yourself, and your world, are the projected images of your mind. The more that we can adopt the characteristics of pure consciousness, the more we can successfully manifest.

Because everyone is at a different level of self-awareness, the next chapter will focus on techniques that most people can identify with. In Chapter 3, we will discuss advanced techniques for challenging your beliefs and perceptions of being a separate self and provide you the opportunity to explore deeper levels of awareness. Ultimately, it's the realization of who you are at the most fundamental level that will allow you to take your manifestation ability to a whole new level.

The entire universe is a great theatre of mirrors.

– Alice Bailey

Chapter 2: Lower-Level Teachings

The lower the level of our resistance, the higher the frequency of our life condition will be for manifesting.

This understanding dates back to the origin of religion. There are fundamental tenets that have been exposed by most, if not all religious traditions that can guide us in lowering our resistance. These tenets were proposed by the original teachers of the religions that we know today, such as Jesus and the Buddha. The reason why these teachers exposed these tenets is because they understood that all of our sufferings could be relieved by lowering our resistance and raising the frequency of our life condition.

The tenets that I speak of are not a mystery. Most of us have been taught of their importance since we were children. They include forgiveness, appreciation, humbleness, gratitude, intention, and service to others.

In addition to these tenets, I have added the unity or oneness of life. Though this tenet may be less known, it is implicit to all the other tenets. The following is what the Bible says of these tenets:

- **Forgiveness:** *But I tell you, love your enemies and pray for those who persecute you.* Matthew 5:43
- **Appreciation or Gratitude:** *Make a joyful noise unto the LORD, all ye lands.* Psalm 100
- **Humbleness:** *Be completely humble and gentle; be patient, bearing with one another in love.* Ephesians 4:2
- **Intention***: Turn from evil and do good; seek peace and pursue it.* Psalm 34:14
- **Service to others:** *Feed the hungry, and help those in trouble. Then your light will shine out from the darkness, and the darkness around you will be as bright as noon.* Isaiah 58:10
- **Oneness:** *On that day you will know that I am in My Father, and you are in Me, and I am in you.* John 14:20

The fact that these tenets are universal points to the mutual understanding by the founders of the world's religions. These founders understood the manifestation process. However, their true intent was often misconstrued when their teachings were transcribed into writings. What was intended to be a parable was taken literally. The wisdom that was attributed to Jesus or the Buddha exists within the depth of the lives of each one of us. Learning to manifest is about getting in touch with the part of ourselves which is universal.

Manifesting is the natural outcome of a vibrational universe where all of existence has a vibrational quality to it. Imagine the strings of a guitar, violin, or any other stringed instrument. Each string vibrates at a specific frequency, which is why each string creates a unique sound. The tighter the string is, the higher the frequency of the sound that it creates. Conversely, the looser the string is, the lower the frequency of its sound. Just as with the guitar string, everything in this universe has its own frequency, which is a result of the how energetic its vibration is.

Another example of the universe's vibrational nature is that of electromagnetic waves, waves that affect every aspect of our lives. Electromagnetic waves form a spectrum of various energy levels, and each energy level has its own quality. When electromagnetic waves vibrate at a very high frequency, they create gamma rays, x-rays, and ultraviolet light. In the middle of the spectrum, we find visible light, and at the lower end of the spectrum, we find microwaves and radio waves. Gamma rays can be used to treat cancer. X-rays make it possible for doctors to identify bone fractures. Ultraviolet light, while invisible, is the light that comes from the sun. We use it to disinfect, stimulate the production of Vitamin D, and get tanned. Microwaves make it possible to cook foods using a microwave oven while radio waves make it possible for us to listen to the radio. The only difference between all of these electromagnetic waves is their frequency.

Just as we cannot get a tan by exposing ourselves to gamma rays, or listen to the radio using visible light, we cannot attract what we want if our lives are not at the right vibrational level. It's the vibrational nature of the universe that makes the Law of Attraction operate.

We attract into our lives that which is a vibrational match to our own lives. What determines our vibrational level is our level of resistance toward life and ourselves, and our resistance is created by our minds, meaning the ego.

At the beginning of this chapter, we discussed the tenets of forgiveness, appreciation, humbleness, gratitude, intention, service to others, and oneness of existence. These tenets work toward lowering our resistance while raising our vibrational level.

We will discuss the significance of each of these tenets in the manifestation process, which will be followed by practical ways to apply them in your daily life. But before we go on to discuss these tenets, we need to backtrack to my earlier statement that we are always manifesting. By understanding this statement, you will grasp what it means to be a "conscious manifester."

With every intention we have, we manifest something into our life. Because most of us are not aware of this, we may believe that we have difficulty manifesting. In truth, we cannot avoid manifesting. We are manifesting without being aware of it! Rather than questioning our ability to manifest, a better question would be how we can take greater control of the manifestation process so that we attract what we desire, rather than that which was unintended. The following discussion of the tenets will explain how they serve us in taking control of our manifestations.

It is the combination of thought and love which forms the
irresistible force of the law of attraction.

– Charles Hammel

Forgiveness

One of the key aspects of using the Law of Attraction is learning to lower our resistance. Resistance refers to when we do not accept a thought, feeling, emotion, other people, situation, or event.

Whenever we resist anything in life, we are giving it our attention. When we do not forgive others for their actions, we give our attention to those thoughts, emotions, and feelings that we have for the situation. The emotions of anger or resentment that we hold onto receive ongoing nourishment from the attention that we provide them. With time, these emotions will manifest themselves as disorders within the body, disorders of the mind, and they will become the overriding force that cancels our conscious attempts to manifest that which we desire.

Our intentions to attract that which we desire are based on our conscious level of thinking. However, the depth of those emotions that we hold onto, due to not forgiving, may become subconscious. At the subconscious level, our inability to forgive will turn on us. If we hang on to the emotions of anger or resentment, they will infiltrate our sense of self. At this stage, manifestations of physical and mental disorders start taking root. That said, this does not mean that you should forgive when you are not ready to, as that can be a source of problems as well.

If we feel pressured to forgive when we do not feel like it, then we are also creating resistance. Not only are we creating resistance, we are dishonoring our own feelings, which will also hamper our ability to consciously manifest and cause us to lose alignment within ourselves.

We lower our resistance when we learn to forgive, as the adage states: Forgiveness is more for the sake of the forgiver than it is for the forgiven. In short, not forgiving others, and attempting to forgive when we are not ready, will create major problems manifesting, especially the manifestations of happiness, self-trust, and well-being.

So how do we walk this tightrope of forgiveness? We honor ourselves by learning to listen to our feelings. If you are not ready to forgive, do not try to change how you feel. However, when you feel ready to move on, here are some suggestions on how to release your resistance:

Exercises

Journal Writing

1. Start keeping a journal and write in it daily. You can use this journal for all of the exercises that we will be discussing. Starting with the tenet of forgiveness, journal about the things that have angered or hurt you. When you write, write from the heart and just let the words flow. Don't intellectualize this exercise. When you think of these upsetting situations, do not think of forgiveness yet. For this step, you are just getting your feelings out on paper.

2. Once you have written out all your feelings about the situation, write out how you would have liked the situation to have turned out. For example, if you just wrote about a situation where someone said or did something that hurt you, I want you to write out how you wished the situation would have went.

3. After writing out how you wished the situation turned out, I want you to think about what may have caused the other person to act the way they did toward you. Remember, the only reason anyone would hurt another person is because they are fearful and experiencing pain themselves.

4. Using your understanding, write some reasons that this person may be fearful or in pain.
5. Next, reflect on the possibility that the other person did not intend to hurt you. Is it possible that your feeling hurt may be a misunderstanding on your part? Write all the reasons why this may be or may not be a possibility.
6. Your final step is to write down what you have learned from this experience and how you may have benefited from it.
7. Review your journal the following day and then five days after that. After reviewing your writings, did you experience any new insights? If you did not, that is okay. If you did get new insights, write those down in your journal as well.

Doing this journal exercise will help you process your experiences rather than keeping them inside you or acting out in a reactive manner. The next exercise can be used to change your beliefs about forgiveness.

Exercise

Belief Balance Sheet: Forgiveness

Do the following:

1. Get three sheets of paper. Select paper that is 8" x 11" or larger.
2. On the first paper, write down the beliefs that that are preventing you from forgiving. The following are examples:

   - If I forgive him, he will feel like he is off the hook.
   - If I forgive her, she may do it again.
   - If I forgive him, it means that it was never that important.
   - To forgive is to be weak.
   - If I forgive, I will open myself to future abuse.

3. Select the one belief that you believe is the biggest reason why you are unable to forgive.
4. Take the second sheet of paper and fold it in half lengthwise.
5. On the top of the paper, write down the belief that you selected.

6. Make a list on the left-hand side of the paper of all the ways this belief has cost you in your life. How has this belief cost you regarding how you feel about yourself? How has it affected your relationships, health, or finances?

7. When writing, keep in mind the following:

   - When writing this list, write down the first thing that comes to your mind, even if it seems irrelevant.

   - Write as fast as you can and feel the emotions that arise. This is a heartfelt exercise, not a cerebral one.

   - Keep writing until you run out of things to write.

8. Next to each item you write down, assign an arbitrary point value to how much impact the item has had on you. When selecting the point value, choose the first number that comes to mind.

9. When you have completed assigning the point values, find the total of all the point values and place it at the bottom of the page.

10. For the right side of the page, repeat Steps 6-8, except this time, write down all of the ways that this belief has benefited you.

When you have completed Step 10, think of a new alternative belief that empowers you. For example, if the original belief was, "If I forgive him, he will feel like he is off the hook," your new belief may be, "Forgiving him may lead him to feel that he is off the hook, but I will be free from this weight that I am carrying around."

On the third paper, repeat steps 4-9 using your new belief, with the following exceptions: Reverse Steps 6 and 9 by writing down all the ways that you believe that you would benefit from this new belief for Step 6. When doing Step 9, write down all the ways you believe it will cost you.

When you have completed the two sheets, do the following:

1. Immediately review your lists, allowing yourself to fully experience any emotions that arise.
2. Review yours lists every day, once in the morning and once before you go to bed, until you become fully associated with the emotions that you experience.

When you become fully associated with the costs for holding on to your old belief with the benefits of adopting your new belief, your mind will become programmed with your new belief.

As soon as you start to feel differently about what you already have, you will start to attract more of the good things, more of the things you can be grateful for.

– Joe Vitale

Appreciation

To understand the power of appreciation in manifesting, we first need to discuss energy levels and identification. Everything in this universe is composed of energy.

At the atomic level, there is just energetic potential. Our emotions are an expression of energy, and each emotion has its own frequency. Emotions such as fear or anger have lower frequencies, while love and appreciation are of a higher frequency level.

Our essential nature is that of energy as well, and as with emotions, we experience different frequencies as well. The frequency of our life force is dependent upon the degree that we identify with our minds and bodies. In periods of deep sleep, we lose all sense of identification with our minds and bodies. During these times, we return to our essential nature, which is pure consciousness or energy. During deep sleep, our vibrational nature is at its highest.

When we identify with our minds and bodies, our vibrational level is lowered. Our lower vibration leads us to experience a sense of separation. We see ourselves as being our minds and bodies, and everything else as being separate from ourselves.

Nurture great thoughts, for you will never go higher than your thoughts.

– Benjamin Disraeli

When we experience the emotions of anger or fear, it is due to the feeling that our sense of self is being threatened. We think things like "I will become angry if you take my money because that was 'my money.' If I lose my job, I will become fearful that I may experience unpleasant consequences to my lifestyle. In both anger and fear, I feel threatened by external events or situations, which I believe will lead to me losing something."

It is not just anger or fear that appears as a result of our sense of identification with the mind and body. Even the emotions of peace or happiness are dependent upon my external world meeting my expectations. If my life is being good to me, I will feel peace or happiness. My peace and happiness will only last as long as things go my way. As soon as life takes a turn, I will experience anger, fear, or any of the other lower vibratory emotions.

The emotion of appreciation is different from the other emotions in that we can experience appreciation without any expectations of receiving anything. It is for this reason that appreciation is considered second only to love in its vibratory level. Appreciation allows us to lose our identification, if only momentarily, with our mind and body, and focus on something outside ourselves.

Since we manifest that which is of the same vibration as our lives, living in appreciation allows us to manifest those experiences which mirror the same high energy level. Appreciation reduces resistance because we are experiencing a connection with something outside ourselves without expecting anything in return. The following exercises will help to cultivate your sense of appreciation:

Exercises

Appreciation Journal

Each day in your journal, write down all of the things that you are, or could be, appreciative of. For each item, write down why you are appreciative for it.

Real-Time Appreciation

Throughout the day each day, take the time to be aware of everything that you are, or could be, appreciative of. The more you do this in a sincere way, the more you will develop your appreciation "muscle."

When it comes to this or any of the other exercises, do not get hung up on looking for major reasons why you should feel a certain way.

Take appreciation as an example. You could be appreciative for the way the sunlight shines on the water of a pond. Such appreciation is just as powerful as having appreciation for having your dreams answered.

The sense of appreciation is what counts, for it is your connection to your higher self. That which you are appreciative of is but a stimulus that triggers your appreciative response. If you have trouble experiencing appreciation, the following exercise may be helpful.

Belief Balance Sheet: Appreciation

1. Get three sheets of paper. Select paper 8" x 11" or larger.

2. On the first paper, write down the beliefs that that are preventing you from feeling appreciation.

3. Select the one belief that you believe is most preventing you from experiencing a sense of appreciation.

4. Fold the second sheet of paper in half lengthwise.

5. At the top of the paper, write down the belief that you selected.

6. Make a list on the left side of the paper of all the ways this belief has cost you in your life. How has this belief cost you in terms of how you feel about yourself? How has it affected your relationships, health, or finances? When writing, keep in mind the following:

   - Write down the first thing that comes to your mind, even if it seems irrelevant.

   - Write as fast as you can and feel the emotions that arise. This is a heartfelt exercise, not a cerebral one.

   - Keep writing until you run out of things to write.

7. Next to each item you write down, assign an arbitrary point value as to how much impact this item has had on you. When selecting the point value, choose the first number that comes to mind.

8. When you have completed assigning the point values, find the total of all the point values and place it at the bottom of the page.

9. For the right side of the page, repeat Steps 6-8, except this time, you will write down all the ways that this belief has benefited you.

When you have completed Step 9, think of a new alternative belief that empowers you.

On the third paper, repeat steps 4-9 using your new belief, with the following exceptions: Reverse Steps 6 and 9 by writing down all the ways that you believe that you would benefit from this new belief for Step 6. When doing Step 9, write down all the ways you believe it will cost you.

When you have completed the two sheets, do the following:

1. Immediately review your lists, allowing yourself to fully experience any emotions that arise.
2. Review yours lists every day, once in the morning and once before you go to bed, until you become fully associated with the emotions that you experience.

When you become fully associated with the costs for holding on to your old belief with the benefits of adopting your new belief, your mind will become programmed with your new belief.

Another approach is to experience greater appreciation is to go inward through the use of meditation:

Appreciation Meditation

1. Find a place where there is minimal distraction and is comfortable. Sit down in a chair or on a pillow, whichever is most comfortable for you.

2. Close your eyes and place your attention on your breathing as you breathe normally.

3. Place your awareness on the sensations that you experience as your breath enters your body during inhalation and leaves it during exhalation.

4. Allow yourself to experience everything that arises in your awareness without any form of judgment or resistance. Greet every experience with complete acceptance.

5. Anytime you find yourself becoming distracted, gently return your awareness back to your breath.

6. Everything that you experience is an opportunity to express appreciation:

   - You can experience appreciation for a person, a pet, or for nature.

   - You can express appreciation for the fact that you can experience thought, sensation, sound, and mental images.

   - You can express appreciation for your breath, which flows through you without any effort on your part, and is essential to your survival.

7. Allow yourself to witness every experience that arises in your awareness without judging, identifying, or analyzing it. Can you find appreciation for the thoughts, sensations, or feelings that you experience as being uncomfortable? Whatever appears before you, allow it to manifest in your awareness without any interference by you.

8. Should you find yourself reacting to any of your experiences, allow yourself to be a witness to your reactions without any form of judgment.

9. When you find yourself experiencing appreciation, try to intensify that feeling. Place your awareness on the feeling of appreciation. Does the feeling of appreciation have a color, texture, or sound? What happens when you focus on the feelings of appreciation? You can use this technique to intensify any emotion or feeling that you experience.

10. Allow yourself to experience the feeling of appreciation as deeply as possible.

11. If you have trouble with this exercise, keep practicing it until you experience the level of appreciation that you desire.

Take the first step in faith. You don't have to see the whole staircase. Just take the first step.

— Dr Martin Luther King Jr.

Humbleness

The value of humbleness in manifesting is, just as with appreciation, that you are creating distance between yourself and your ego. Appreciation causes us to focus outside ourselves. Being humble downplays the feeling of self-importance while being appreciative of the value that others offer.

Being humble is a position of strength. The humble person does not have to defend or prove themselves. Conversely, those who are connected to their ego exert a great deal of energy defending themselves or trying to persuade others to see their point of view. Anytime we attempt to persuade others to adopt our point of view, or become attached to an image of ourselves, we create resistance. We are creating resistance because we do not feel secure enough to allow others to hold an opposing point of view. We create resistance when we have to hold on to a self-image out of fear of being insignificant.

From an intellectual or societal perspective, the thing that we want to avoid at all costs is appearing insignificant. From the perspective of higher levels of consciousness, being insignificant is a victory over the ego.

With humbleness, self-importance is diminished. The ego is the source of resistance; being humble requires creating distance from the ego. If you feel that you have problems feeling humble, do the following exercise:

Exercises

Belief Balance Sheet: Humbleness

Do the following:

1. Get three sheets of paper. Select paper 8" x 11" or larger.
2. On the first paper, write down the beliefs that that are preventing you from feeling humble.
3. Select the one belief that you believe is the biggest reason why you are unable to feel humble.
4. Take the second sheet of paper and fold it in half lengthwise.
5. On the top of the paper, write down the belief that you selected.
6. Make a list on the left side of the paper of all the ways this belief has cost you in your life. When writing, keep in mind the following:

- When writing this list, write down the first thing that comes to your mind, even if it seems irrelevant.
- Write as fast as you can and feel the emotions that arise. This is a heartfelt exercise, not a cerebral one.
- Keep writing until you cannot think of what to write.

7. Next to each item you write down, assign an arbitrary point value as to how much impact this item has had on you. When selecting the point value, choose the first number that comes to mind.

8. When you have completed assigning the point values, find the total of all the point values and place it at the bottom of the page.

9. For the right side of the page, repeat Steps 5-7, except this time, you will write down all the ways that this belief has benefited you.

When you have completed Step 9, think of a new empowering belief to replace your old belief. On the third paper, repeat steps 4-9 using your new belief with the following exceptions: Reverse Steps 6 and 9 by writing down all the ways that you believe that you would benefit from this new belief for Step 6. When doing Step 9, write down all the ways you believe it will cost you.

When you have completed the two sheets, do the following:

1. Immediately review your lists, allowing yourself to fully experience any emotions that arise.
2. Review yours lists every day, once in the morning and once before you go to bed, until you become fully associated with the emotions that you experience.

When you become fully associated with the costs for holding on to your old belief with the benefits of adopting your new belief, your mind will become programmed with your new belief.

Gratitude is an attitude that hooks us up to our source of supply. And the more grateful you are, the closer you become to your maker, to the architect of the universe, to the spiritual core of your being. It's a phenomenal lesson.

– Bob Proctor

Gratitude

In an earlier chapter, it was indicated that the emotion of appreciation was second only to love in vibrational level. Gratitude is ranked below appreciation only because we are normally grateful because we have received something. The state of gratefulness is dependent upon our external conditions. I may feel grateful because I have a job, my health, or because I received a gift. If I lose any of these things, I could easily move from gratefulness to fear or anger. On the other hand, losing these things may lead me to experience a sense of appreciation for what I once had, or what I may have learned as a result of it.

My sense of appreciation is not dependent on my external conditions while gratitude is. However, having gratitude is still important for manifesting. If we lack gratitude, we are experiencing resistance. We are practicing resistance because we feel that our current situation is not good enough. If I feel that my current situation is not good enough, then I am resisting the present moment. Finally, if I resist the present moment, I am in resistance to all that is, including myself.

The power of the spirit of gratitude is that it leads us to accept the present moment as opposed to thinking of how we want things to be. Focusing on what we want without acceptance of the present moment will lead us to manifest more of that which we don't want. Gratitude reduces resistance by causing us to focus on what we have. By expressing gratitude, we are focusing on the present moment versus thinking of lack or of greener pastures in the future.

Exercises

Gratitude Journal

Each day in your journal, write down all the things that you are or could be grateful for. For each item that you write down, write down why you are grateful for it.

Real-Time Gratitude

Each day, take time to become aware of anything that you are or could be grateful for. The more you do this in a sincere way, the more you will develop your gratitude "muscle." When looking for things to be grateful for, consider everything, not just the typical response that others give. In other words, you could be grateful that the sun is shining, for the kindness of others, or for your manifested form that allows you to experience life.

What counts is the developing of a sense of gratitude, because gratitude, along with the other higher frequency emotions, indicates alignment between our manifested self and our higher version. That which you are grateful for is but a stimulus that triggers your grateful response.

Belief Balance Sheet: Gratefulness

If you feel that you have problems feeling gratefulness, do the following:

1. Get three sheets of paper. Select paper 8" x 11" or larger.
2. On the first paper, write down the beliefs that that are preventing you from feeling grateful.
3. Select the one belief that you believe is the biggest reason why you are not experiencing the feeling of gratefulness.
4. Take the second sheet of paper and fold it in half lengthwise.
5. On the top of the paper, write down the belief that you selected.

6. Make a list on the left hand side of the paper of all the ways this belief has cost you in your life. How has this belief cost you in terms of how you feel about yourself? How has it affected your relationships, health, or finances? When writing, keep in mind the following:
    - Write down the first thing that comes to your mind, even if it seems irrelevant.
    - Write as fast as you can and feel the emotions that arise. This is a heartfelt exercise, not a cerebral one.
    - Keep writing until you run out of things to write.
7. By each item you write down, assign an arbitrary point value as to how much impact the item has had on you. When selecting the point value, choose the first number that comes to mind.
8. When you have completed assigning the point values, find the total of all the point values and place it at the bottom of the page.
9. For the right side of the page, repeat Steps 6-8, except this time, write down all the ways that this belief has benefited you.
10. When you have completed Step 9, think of a new alternative belief that empowers you.

When you have completed Step 9, think of a new empowering belief to replace your old belief. On the third paper, repeat steps 4-9 using your new belief, with the following exceptions: Reverse Steps 6 and 9 by writing down all the ways that you believe that you would benefit from this new belief for Step 6. When doing Step 9, write down all the ways you believe it will cost you.

When you have completed the two sheets, do the following:

1. Immediately review your lists, allowing yourself to fully experience any emotions that arise.
2. Review yours lists every day, once in the morning and once before you go to bed, until you become fully associated with the emotions that you experience.

When you become fully associated with the costs for holding on to your old belief with the benefits of adopting your new belief, your mind will become programmed with your new belief.

Service to Others

Regardless of the culture or religious teaching, the concept of service is a central tenant. In recovery groups, such as Alcoholics Anonymous, service to others is an integral part of the program. The reason why service to others is so entrenched in our society is that, like any other spiritual or ethical principle, it creates distance between us and our ego. By creating distance, we release resistance. When acting in the service of others, our focus shifts from our ego to the well-being of others.

Exercises

Journaling

1. In your journal, do the following:
2. Make a list of all the things that you enjoy doing.
3. Make a list of your skills, talents, and things which you are knowledgeable about.
4. Make list of all the needs that you are aware of that are being experienced by your family, community, state, or country.
5. Reflect on how you can integrate Steps 1-3 into serving those you indicated in Step 4.

For example, someone may identify relationship skills, artistic ability, and marketing as their strengths. They also may have identified neighborhood blight as a problem in their community.

This person could serve their community by organizing a group of people to beautify their neighborhood by removing graffiti or creating murals and other forms of artwork for people to enjoy.

Using their knowledge of marketing, they would be able to create partnerships with the business community for support and needed resources.

It is true that you could skip this exercise and just find a way to serve others. The advantage of doing this exercise is that by aligning your gifts and abilities, you can create even a greater impact for those you are serving, as well as for yourself.

Whatever the mind can conceive it can achieve.

– W. Clement Stone

Intention

Of all the factors that influence our ability to manifest, one of the most fundamental is intention. Being able to consciously manifest requires our intentions to be toward creating value or happiness for others. As long as our intentions are to serve ourselves, or harm others, we will continue to create suffering for ourselves and others. Such intentions are the result of fear, and the only things that fear manifests are more fear and suffering. Conversely, having intentions to create value or happiness for others brings a higher frequency to our lives, which will attract manifestations of like kind.

Exercise

Creative Intentions

Start checking in with yourself before making a decision that impacts others or the environment by doing the following:

1. Before making your decision, consider all of your options. For each option, consider its potential impact on all stakeholders, including you.
   - Does the option being considered benefit you at the expense of others?
   - Does the option being considered benefit others at your own expense?

The ideal option benefits all stakeholders. The problem most people experience during decision making is that they have not put enough time or creativity into coming up with options. We are very rarely restricted to only two options when it comes to decision making.

With thoughtful reflection and creativity, we can usually come up with a number of options by taking different elements of our initial options and combining them to create new options. Use this process to find an option that provides the greatest benefits for all involved.

By doing this process, you will move from a fear-based and limited perspective and toward a holistic perspective, which will lower your resistance.

Meditation

The following meditation can be practiced to use the body's wisdom when making a decision:

1. Sit down and make yourself comfortable.
2. Close your eyes and place your attention on your breath as it travels in and out of your body during inhalation and exhalation.
3. If you become distracted, return your attention back to your breath.
4. Continue focusing on your breath until your mind becomes calm and you are aware of the sensations of the body.
5. When you have reached the state described in Step 4, consider each option of your decision. As you consider each option, pay close attention to how your body

responds when you consider the particular option. Examples of the body's reactions may include:

- Tightening or loosening of your chest
- Shallow breathing or breathing more fully.
- Your body feeling heavy or light.
- Tension or relaxation

6. The option that you want to choose is the one that gives you the greatest sense of well-being.

7. If you find that your breath is shallow, your chest is tight, or your body feels tense, then that option is not the option that you should choose.

8. It may be necessary to practice this meditation until you become more aware of the body's sensations, and you can determine how your body responds when contemplating your options.

How wonderful it is that nobody need wait a single moment before starting to improve the world.

– Anne Frank

Oneness of Existence

Oneness is often referenced in spiritual teachings. However, it remains just a concept for most of us. Our experience of life is anything but oneness, with all of its diversity. Besides diversity, we also experience ourselves as separate beings amidst all of this diversity. Unless you practice meditation or some other deep contemplative practice, the experience of oneness will remain conceptual.

A heartfelt understanding of Oneness dissolves the feeling of separateness. Though our sensory experience will continue to give the impression of separateness, our sense of personhood will dissolve as we merge with our experience of life.

In deep sleep, nothing is experienced because there is only awareness. To be devoid of experience is to encounter the essence of Oneness. If there is only Oneness, what is there to attract or manifest? We are projections of pure consciousness that have manifested for the purpose of being able to experience. It is through our experiencing that pure consciousness experiences itself.

By moving toward the direction of Oneness, we can enjoy the best of both worlds. We can enjoy our manifested selves while tapping into our un-manifested selves.

In the next chapter, you will have an opportunity to engage in a powerful meditation to gain a more intuitive understanding of your un-manifested self. For now, here is a more intellectual exercise for understanding oneness. Before presenting this exercise, it is necessary to provide an example of how you can perceive oneness in everyday life.

If we look at a tree, we will most likely perceive the tree as being a separate entity unto itself. The tree is seen as being a separate entity from all the other entities. We do not confuse the tree for a rock, a bird, or for ourselves. We see the tree as being a fixed entity, and the tree will never be anything but a tree. Further, we will most likely believe that the tree is made of tree parts, those aspects that constitute the tree. The "tree parts" could be its leaves, trunk, bark, and roots. This view of the tree is a dualistic view in that we see the tree as a separate entity unto itself that is comprised of "tree parts."

Divine mind is the one and only reality.

– Charles Fillmore

If we reflect more deeply, however, we can see that this dualistic view of the tree is just an illusion. The sun provides the light that the tree needs to conduct photosynthesis. Without the sun, the tree could not exist.

The carbon dioxide molecules that are a component of the air are needed by the tree for it to conduct photosynthesis. Without the carbon dioxide molecule, there could be no tree. Clouds produce rain which the tree depends upon for its water. Without the clouds, the tree could not exist.

The nutrients in soil are absorbed by the tree's roots. Without the soil, the tree could not exist. From the perspective oneness, the tree is made of the sun, carbon dioxide molecules, clouds, and soil.

This is just a simplified example, and there are numerous other entities that make the existence of the tree possible. In turn, all of the entities that make the existence of the tree possible are themselves dependent upon other entities for their existence.

If there was no evaporation of water, clouds could not exist. If there were no electrical charges, the carbon dioxide molecule could not exist, and so on. Ultimately, the tree is not a separate entity unto itself. Rather, the tree is the composite of the entire universe. The entire universe creates the tree, and the tree is a testimony to the existence of the universe.

There is no such thing as a "tree;" rather, what we call "tree" is the composite of the totality of existence.

We believe in the Law of Attraction because we have a dualistic view of ourselves and our place in this universe. However, just as with the tree, you are the composite of all of existence.

Many of the elements that your body is made of originated from the stars, while your body has the same salt concentration as ocean water. Every aspect of who you are is the result of the existence of something else. Any sense of being a separate and distinct entity unto yourself is just an illusion. Any doubts or challenges that you may feel that you have in manifesting are just illusions. That which you are trying to attract is an aspect of you already. Instead of thinking that you are in the universe, it would be more accurate to say that the universe is found within you.

This statement will hopefully become more apparent in the next chapter. For now, try this exercise:

Meditation

1. Sit down and make yourself comfortable.
2. Close your eyes and place your attention on your breath as travels in and out of your body during inhalation and exhalation.
3. If you become distracted, return your attention back to your breath.
4. When your mind is calm, open your eyes and find an object to look at. The object that you look at can be living or non-living.
5. As you look at the object, refrain from engaging in any form of judgment.
6. As you study the object, ask yourself the following questions:
7. Is there any aspect of this object that is not subject to change? (Example: If you are viewing a flower, you know that the flower is subject to change due to the seasons and its life span.)
8. How is the object that you are observing impacted by the other objects in its environment? Example: Insects and birds make it possible for pollination of the flower to occur.

9. Meditate on how the object of your observation owes its existence to other seemingly unrelated objects.

When one door of happiness closes, another opens; but often we look so long at the closed door that we do not see the one which has been opened for us.

– Helen Keller

Chapter 3: Upper-Level Teachings

In this chapter, you will find exercises that are more advanced than those in the previous chapter, as well as more detailed information about the topic of resistance.

Resistance

Just as with guitar strings or electromagnetic waves, the life of each one of us has its own frequency or vibrational level. Our frequency is dependent upon on the amount of resistance that is in our lives.

The less resistance we have, the higher the frequency of our lives. The higher the frequency, the more efficiently we can conscientiously manifest. The lower the frequency we have, the less ability we have to manifest that which we desire. The reason for this is that the resistance we hold receives a greater amount of our attention than that which we want to manifest.

Since what we focus on is what we manifest, we attract more of that which we are resistant to. What is it that we are resisting? We are resisting our higher nature, which is pure consciousness. Anytime we resist anything, we are going against our essential nature.

We are simultaneously nonphysical and physical beings at the same time. As a physical being, we have forgotten our true nature. Because we have forgotten our true nature, we experience resistance to anything that we perceive to be threatening to our sense of self.

If we realized that our true nature is that of consciousness, nothing could pose a threat to us. Since we would not perceive anything as a threat, we would not generate resistance. It is the lack of resistance that allows pure conscious to manifest as existence.

Whenever we do not accept the present moment, we create resistance. When we look toward the future, because we feel the present is not sufficient, we are creating resistance. When we lament the past, we are not accepting the present moment. When we are preoccupied with what may happen in the future, we are not accepting the present moment.

Nothing is, unless our thinking makes it so.

– Shakespeare

Resistance can even occur while manifesting, even when we have the best intentions. The following personal story will illustrate this. When I first practiced manifesting, I made the intention that I would see a certain book cover when I went to the library later that day.

To my pleasant surprise, I saw the exact book cover that I visualized upon arriving there. The following day, I decided to manifest something else. I made the intention that during that day, I would encounter a purple circular object with red spots. Throughout the day I looked for the object, but it never appeared. Why was my second attempt to manifest a disappointment when my first day was a complete success? There could be a number of factors. However, the primary factor was my own resistance. On my first manifestation attempt, I simply made my intention, forgot about it, and went on with my day. On my second attempt, I made my intention, but I did not forget about it. Instead of going on with my day, I kept looking for my manifestation to appear.

Every time I looked and did not see it, I started to experience doubt. My sense of doubt was a form of resistance. On my first attempt, I forgot about my intentions and just went on with my day. My manifestation appeared before me when I was not looking for it. The concept of detachment is frequently discussed in spiritual teachings. My first manifestation attempt was successful because I was detached from the outcome of my intentions, unlike on my second day.

The following are recommendations for becoming detached to your outcome:

1. If you are not already experienced in manifesting, start practicing your manifesting abilities by making your intentions about things that are inconsequential to you. If you do not have an emotional connection to your intention, your ego will not get involved. Continue creating intentions that do not have significance for you. As your manifestations take place, you can gradually make more relevant intentions.

2. Practice the meditations in this book until you start intuitively experiencing the understanding that who you are is the one that is aware, or the knower of all of experience. By reaching this level of awareness, your thoughts of doubt will lose their ability to influence you.

One of the most important practices to develop to be a successful manifester is that of meditation or mindfulness. Meditation and mindfulness practices allow us to develop greater attention to the present moment and to be less distracted by our thoughts. When we become less identified with our thoughts, we release our resistance to them.

Think of a time when you could not remember a person's name. At that moment, you were experiencing a thought, the idea that you had forgotten the person's name. This thought may have led to a sense of uneasiness, which was created by another thought, the thought that you should know their name. Because this feeling consumed your attention, you continued to struggle to remember their name.

It is attention that energizes our thoughts; thoughts within themselves are powerless. When we energize our thoughts, they become manifested in our life. The more you tried to remember their name, the more frustrated you became. You fully manifested the experience of forgetting the other person's name.

In your frustration, you may have given up on trying to remember their name. When that happened, you removed your attention from the chain of thoughts that you created, resulting in them losing their power. Because of this, your memory of their name returned soon afterward.

Just as in my personal story about manifesting, I held no attachments to my outcome of manifesting on the first day, but became fully attached on the second day.

When a thought becomes the attraction point for similar thoughts, as described in the scenario of remembering a name, that thought becomes emboldened by the attention that we give it. The potency of these thoughts gives us a sense of certainty to their truthfulness. When we are confident that our thoughts are true, we have created what is commonly known as a "belief."

All that we are is a result of what we have thought.

– Buddha

Belief systems:

Our beliefs determine our experience of life, and our beliefs are like filters through which we experience the world. Beliefs are like tinted sunglasses that we have forgotten that we have on. Whatever color lens we have on will be how we experience the world. To not be aware of our beliefs, and not question them, is probably the single most important reason for us having trouble taking control of the manifestation process.

Our beliefs determine what we think, notice, do not notice, the actions that we take, and how we experience the world and ourselves. If a person has the belief that other people cannot be trusted, then that person's focus will be on all the reasons why other people cannot be trusted.

Not only will their focus be on why other people cannot be trusted, but they also will not notice any information that supports the contrary. Because of this, all of this person's actions will be based on the belief that people cannot be trusted, and they will experience the world as a risky place. Additionally, they will see themselves as being guarded.

Cherish your visions and your dreams as they are the children of your soul, the blueprints of your ultimate achievements.

– Napoleon Hill

It is the power of beliefs that prevent us from experiencing our unlimited potential to manifest. Holding the belief that you cannot be a successful manifester will result in your inability to manifest consciously, which will prevent you from taking charge of the manifesting process.

You will not notice everything that you are manifesting, believing that their appearance is the result of coincidence or luck. Similarly, you will attribute your undesirable experiences to bad luck, fate, or destiny.

How attached we are to our beliefs determines if we see ourselves as separate beings who are trying to manifest our desires or whether we come to the recognition that who we are is inseparable from all of existence.

What you radiate outward in your thoughts, feelings, mental pictures and words, you attract into your life.

– Catherine Ponder

When we identify with our minds and bodies, we cannot help but believe that we lack something in our life. It is this very sense of lack that leads us to the Law of Attraction or some other teachings.

When we learn to practice complete acceptance of all of our experiences, we release our sense of resistance. When we release our sense of resistance, we may come to the realization that who we are is beyond anything that we can experience.

When we realize that who we are is not what we experience, we may come to the realization that it is impossible to lack anything. Hence, manifesting and the Law of Attraction become totally irrelevant as we recognize that our true nature is that of unlimited potential.

Because the ability to manifest is dependent on how much we identify with our minds and bodies, the remaining portion of this book is devoted to techniques that can be used to move closer to the recognition of our highest self.

Exercise

Belief Balance Sheet: Releasing Intentions

To address any belief that you have that may be preventing you from manifesting to the degree that you want, do the following:

1. Get three sheets of paper. Select paper 8" x 11" or larger.

2. On the first paper, write down the beliefs that are preventing you from manifesting.

3. Select the one belief that you believe is the biggest obstacle to manifesting that which you desire.

4. Fold the second sheet of paper in half lengthwise.

5. At the top of the paper, write down the belief that you selected.

6. Make a list on the left side of the paper of all the ways that this belief has cost you in your life. How has this belief cost you in terms of how you feel about yourself? How has it affected your relationships, health, or finances? When writing, keep in mind the following:

- Write down the first thing that comes to your mind, even if it seems irrelevant.

- Write as fast as you can and feel the emotions that arise. This is a heartfelt exercise, not a cerebral one.

- Keep writing until you run out of things to write.

7. Next to each item you write down, assign an arbitrary point value as to how much impact this item has had on you. When selecting the point value, choose the first number that comes to mind.

8. When you have completed assigning the point values, find the total of all the point values and place it at the bottom of the page.

9. For the right side of the page, repeat Steps 6-8, except this time, you will write down all the ways that this belief has benefited you.

When you have completed Step 9, think of a new alternative belief that empowers you.

On the third paper, repeat steps 4-9 using your new belief with the following exceptions: Reverse Steps 6 and 9 by writing down all the ways that you believe that you would benefit from this new belief for Step 6. When doing Step 9, write down all the ways you believe it will cost you.

When you have completed the two sheets, do the following:

1. Immediately review your lists, allowing yourself to fully experience any emotions that arise.

2. Review yours lists every day, once in the morning and once before you go to bed, until you become fully associated with the emotions that you experience.

When you become fully associated with the costs for holding on to your old belief with the benefits of adopting your new belief, your mind will become programmed with your new belief.

Every single second is an opportunity to change your life, because in any moment you can change the way you feel.

– Rhonda Byrne

Emotions

Our emotions are a mirror to the thoughts that we are thinking. The emotions that we experience are the sensory equivalent of our thoughts, both conscious and subconscious.

We cannot see or feel a thought; there is just an awareness that we are having one. Our emotions, on the other hand, are sensory since we can feel them.

If you are experiencing emotions that are empowering you, it is because you are experiencing thoughts of the same quality. By changing our feelings, we change our thoughts.

The Secret was valuable in introducing people to the Law of Attraction. However, it presented the Law of Attraction in a simple manner.

Like many other Law of Attraction products on the market, the Secret focused on how we can manifest by the thoughts that we hold. While it is true our thoughts are the source of our manifestations, what is not explained is the role that our emotions play.

Imagine that you are trying to manifest money, so you hold on to that intention. At the same time, you are holding on to deep-seated emotions from your past regarding scarcity. Because these emotions are deep-seated, you are not aware of them, except when they rise to the surface during times of uncertainty.

As discussed earlier, everything in this universe has a vibration. Thoughts and emotions become subconscious when we divert our attention from them.

To keep thoughts and feelings at the subconscious level requires the expenditure of a large amount of energy. Because this expenditure of energy is greater than that which is being directed to your intentions, you continue to manifest scarcity instead of money.

Our emotions impact our ability to manifest at the conscious level as well. While our intentions are powerful, what makes them even more powerful is when we become fully associated with the emotions that come from our intention.

While the intention for manifesting more money is powerful, what would be even more powerful is for you to focus on the emotions that you would have if you had the money already.

See the things that you want as already yours. Know that they will come to you at need. Then let them come. Don't fret and worry about them. Don't think about your lack of them. Think of them as yours, as belonging to you, as already in your possession.

– Robert Collier

The following exercise is for employing the power of your emotions in the manifesting process:

Exercises

Harnessing Emotional Power

1. Sit down and make yourself comfortable.
2. Close your eyes and place your attention on your breath as travels in and out of your body during inhalation and exhalation.
3. If you become distracted, return your attention back to your breath.
4. When your mind is calm, bring forth the intention that you wish to manifest.
5. As you think of your intentions, imagine the thing which you desire to attract exists already in your life.
6. In your mind, visualize that which you want to manifest as clearly as possible.
7. Imagine what it would feel like to touch your manifestation.
8. Imagine what you would hear if your intentions were already manifested.
9. If you could taste your manifestation, what would it taste like?
10. How would you feel if your manifested intention was in your life right now? Allow yourself to experience your emotions fully.

11. When you can experience the emotions, intensify them by placing your attention on them.
12. Experience your emotions intensifying. You can stay in this space for as long as you desire.
13. Repeat this focus on your emotions as often as possible when meditating until your manifestations appear.

The following exercise will allow you to transform deep-seated emotions. This next exercise is more advanced in that it requires your willingness to experience unpleasant emotions.

Diving Deep into an Emotion

1. Think of a situation that is bothering you.
2. When you have identified the situation, ask yourself why this situation bothers you.
3. As you think about the situation, become aware of the feelings that you experience.

Continuing with this exercise, we will use an example. In this example, we will use the emotion of anger.

4. Allow yourself to fully experience the anger you feel. As you experience the anger, identify what anger FEELS like. I have emphasized the word *feel* because this

exercise requires that you remain in the experience of feeling, not thinking.

You do not want to involve your mind in this exercise because it will just unleash a bunch of stories about what happened. Instead, ask yourself the question, "What does anger feel like?" When asking this question, pay attention to the first answer that comes to you. Again, do not think about it.

5. Continuing with this example, let us say your response to this question is that when angry, it **feels** like your face is tightening.
6. Your next step is to become fully associated with the feeling of tightening. Allow yourself to dive into this feeling.
7. When you become fully associated with the feeling of tightening, repeat the question by asking, "What does tightening feel like?"
8. Continuing with the example, your answer may be that tightening **feels** hard.
9. Become fully associated with the feeling of hardness; allow yourself to dive into this feeling.
10. When you become fully associated with the feeling of hardness, repeat the question by asking, "What does hardness **feel** like?"

11. Continuing with the example, you may say that hardness has a numbing feeling.
12. Become fully associated with the feeling of numbness; allow yourself to dive into this feeling.
13. Ask yourself "What does numbness **feel** like?"
14. Based on your response, you would continue to ask the question "What does (feeling) feel like?"
15. You would continue with this line of questioning until your start experiencing neutral or positive emotions.

What you accomplish in doing this exercise is the transformation of your feelings and emotions at the conscious and subconscious levels. By continuously placing your awareness on what you are experiencing, fully experiencing it, and identifying it, your experience of emotions and feelings will be transformed. You may experience a return of the original feelings or emotions, which is normal. If you continue to utilize this exercise when they show up, eventually you will gain the upper hand.

Earlier in this book, we discussed the role of separation as to how we experience ourselves. By seeing ourselves as separate entities that inhabit this planet, we create resistance toward those experiences that we find threatening. It is our resistance that interferes with our ability to manifest our desires. The following are advanced exercises to develop a new perspective on your sense separation

Exercise

1. Sit down and make yourself comfortable.

2. Look at an object in your environment.

3. Determine for yourself how is that you know that you are seeing the object.

   Your first response to this question will probably be, "Because I see it!"

   But how do you know that you are seeing? The answer to that question is that you are aware of it. You are aware that seeing is taking place.

4. As you look at the object, determine for yourself whether the process of seeing ends at some point at which the object begins, or does the process of seeing and the object flow into each other?

Hopefully, you have come to the conclusion that the process of seeing and the object flow into each other. We cannot separate seeing from the object being seen.

5. Inquire for yourself as to where seeing takes place. Does seeing originate from within you, or outside of you?

How is that you know that the process of seeing and the object being seen flow into each other? How do you know that the process of seeing occurs from within you? The answer to both of these questions is awareness. You are aware of all of these things.

So far, we can come to the following conclusions:

- The process of seeing and the object being seen flow into each other. They are one in the same.
- The process of seeing occurs from within you.
- The realization of the previous two points was derived from awareness or knowing.

From these conclusions, we can surmise that the object being seen, the process of being seen, and you, the seer, are inseparable from each other. All of these things are known because there is an awareness of it.

We can take this process a step further by inquiring into the nature of who you are. You are the one who observed the object, but how do you know that you exist? You know that you exist because you are aware of that as well. The next logical question would be who or what is aware of you? The answer to that question is the truth of who you are. You can explore this further using the next exercise.

Exercise

Self-Inquiry

1. Sit down and make yourself comfortable.

2. Close your eyes and place your attention on your breath as travels in and out of your body during inhalation and exhalation.

3. If you become distracted, return your attention back to your breath.

4. When your mind becomes calm, allow your attention to roam freely. Do not try to control anything.

5. Allow yourself to become the witness to all that you experience. Receive each experience with complete acceptance. Do not judge, analyze, or try to modify anything that you experience. Let all of your experience come and go on their own accord.

6. As you meditate, you will experience thoughts, perceptions, sensations, and sounds. Notice how they appear into your awareness and then fade away. Observe how they change in their form or intensity. Nothing that you experience remains unchanged.

7. Notice how the mental phenomena you experience carry out their existence without any effort on your part. Thoughts, perceptions, and sensations happen by themselves.

8. Notice that, as the observer of all mental phenomena; you cannot be them. You are not the thoughts,

perceptions, or sensations that you experience. You are the knower of them.

9. Who is the knower of your experience? Who is the one that is aware?

Remember that you are the witness or knower of all of your experiences. Any answer that you come up with as to the question of the identity of knower cannot be correct. How can anything that you experience be the knower if it is also known?

10. Keep looking for the knower, the one that is aware. Can you find it?

Our minds operate conceptually. In other words, our minds can only recognize that which takes on form. Thoughts, perceptions, sensations, sounds, and smells are all recognized by our minds as they can be conceptualized. The truth of who you are, the one who is the knower, the one who is aware, cannot be detected by the mind, for it is non-phenomenal.

Practicing this meditation will result in expanding your awareness to the truth of your existence and the illusionary nature of all of your experiences. Who you are is awareness itself, and as awareness, you are the knower of all experience. Experience owes its existence to you. How can you experience anything unless there is an awareness of it? By confirming this for yourself, you will go a long way to removing your sense of separation from the world around you. When you reduce the potency of your sense of separation, your level of resistance will be reduced. Finally, when you reduce your level of resistance, you will increase your vibrational frequency. The vibrational frequency will allow you to manifest into your life that which you desire.

Nothing external to me has any power over me.

– Walt Whitman

Chapter 4: Making Sense of it All

We have covered a lot of information so far, so in this chapter, we will discuss how to make sense of it all. Before we do this, let us do a quick review:

1. We are multidimensional beings who are both physical and non-physical simultaneously.
2. Our physical self is an expression of our non-physical being, which is pure consciousness.
3. Everything in this universe is of a vibratory nature. It is this vibratory nature that ultimately makes the manifestation process possible. Our physical being is the result of pure consciousness lowering its vibratory level.
4. As physical beings, we are constantly manifesting, though we may be unaware of it. It is this lack of awareness that leads us to attract both desired and undesired circumstances into our life. We attract both because we are unaware that we are the ones that are doing the manifesting.

5. We can increase our ability to manifest that which we desire by placing greater attention on our vibratory level.
6. Our vibratory level is determined by the level of acceptance or resistance that we have within our lives.
7. Resistance leads to a sense of separation, and a sense of separation leads to further resistance.
8. By learning to live with acceptance, gratitude, appreciation, service to others, and forgiveness, we raise our vibration.
9. When we hold on to resistance, we lower our vibration.
10. The quality of our vibration determines what we attract into our lives.
11. To become conscious manifesters, we need to lower our resistance.

Now that we have reviewed the past content, we will now discuss how to use the information presented in this book.

Preparing for Manifesting

As indicated at the beginning of this book, everyone is different in respect to their level of awareness as it relates to their connection with the greater self or the universe. It is for this reason that such a broad spectrum of exercises was provided in this book.

No one exercise in this book is more useful than the rest. What determines the effectiveness of any given exercise is how well it resonates with you. Further, the number of potential practices for raising your vibrational level is endless.

In fact, you do not even need exercises if you are intuitive enough to move beyond your mind and allow yourself to experience the present moment.

Having said all of this, you should use this book similar to a buffet. Try the activities that seem interesting or enjoyable to you, but do not be afraid to try those exercises that seem too simple or esoteric.

Allow yourself to experiment with the exercises that seem to be right for you. Do not worry about how many activities you select to do; there is no precise number. It is important to state that there is an advantage of doing different exercises in that it allows you to experiment with different perspectives. All of the exercises in this book point toward the same thing, which is that you have the ability to take charge of your vibrational level.

A person is what he or she thinks about all day long.

– Ralph Waldo Emerson

Once you have selected the exercises, practice them until you feel comfortable that you have achieved the outcome of the exercise. The results of all of the exercises are the same: Lowering your resistance toward yourself and others and realizing that you can take charge of your vibratory level. How do you know your vibratory level? It is simple. The higher your vibratory level, the more you will experience peacefulness, acceptance, and centeredness.

 This does not mean you never get angry, upset, or have a bad day, for all of these experiences are normal. What will be different is that these experiences will have less of an impact on you.

The second thing that is important to note is that you do not want to let your ego get involved with the practicing of these exercises. It is natural to approach these activities with expectations or judgments. However, this will only engage your ego. When conducting these exercises, approach them as a blank slate, even if you do them daily. Each time you do these exercises; approach them as if you were doing them for the first time.

While doing these exercises, you may experience distracting thoughts, which is okay. Do not attempt to rationalize, deny, or resist any thoughts that may arise. Rather, allow them complete freedom to express themselves, but do not engage with them.

It should be noted that the Belief Balance Sheet occurs in many places in the exercise sections of this book. This exercise's sole purpose is to assist you in identifying the beliefs that may be impeding your ability to manifest and replacing them with more empowering ones. I recommend that you do these exercises in conjunction with any of the meditative practices, particularly for those in the last section.

Doing the Belief Balance Sheet exercises in conjunction with any of the other exercises will create an excellent foundation for manifesting. The Belief Balance Sheet exercises should not be done just one time, they should be done on an ongoing basis so that you are continuously rooting out any disempowering beliefs that you may have.

Unless you have experience in meditation and manifesting, I advise that you start off with the exercises in Chapter 2 before attempting the exercises in Chapter 3. All of the previous meditations in this book were intended to expand your level of awareness to reduce your sense of separation and resistance. The following is the last exercise in this book. It is by no means the most complicated in this book; however, all the previous activities will prepare you to get the most out of it.

Exercise

Meditation for Releasing Your Intention

1. Find a place where there is a minimal amount of distraction. Sit down in a chair or on a pillow, whichever is most comfortable for you.
2. Close your eyes and place your attention on your breath as you breathe normally.
3. Place your awareness on the sensations that you experience as your breath enters your body during inhalation and leaves it during exhalation.
4. Allow yourself to experience everything that arises in your awareness without any form of judgment or resistance. Greet every experience with complete acceptance.
5. Anytime you find yourself becoming distracted, gently return your awareness back to your breath.

With practice, you will be able to extend the amount of time that you can stay focused on your breath. With that focus, you will find your mind getting increasingly calmer. You will continue to experience thoughts.

However, they gradually lose their ability to impact you. Remember, your thoughts derive all of their power from the attention that we give them.

6. When you have thoughts, simply acknowledge their presence and then return your attention to your breath.

7. When your mind is calm, you will notice that your thoughts will slow down, enough that you will be able to recognize the space between your thoughts. In other words, there is a space that exists between the time that one thought fades away and the next one appears.

8. When you have found this space, release your intentions into that space.

9. Follow these steps with each meditation. You can release more than one intention during your meditation.

Practicing meditation and making an intention is easy, not getting caught up in self-doubt as we wait for our manifestation to appear is the difficult part. The key to manifesting is getting in a relaxed state, releasing your intention, and then becoming detached from your outcome. By becoming detached from your outcome, you will not think about it. When you do not think about it, you will not doubt that it will happen. When you do not doubt that it will happen, you will not experience resistance. When you release your resistance, your manifestation will appear when the conditions are right.

If you can dream it, you can do it.

– Walt Disney

Do not get fooled into believing that you can manifest without exerting any effort on your part. While it is true that manifesting without effort is possible, it requires removing your resistance to a minimal level.

Achieving such low levels of resistance requires intensive meditative practices. For most of us, we also need to get actively involved in making our manifestations come true. If you want to manifest a new sports car, and all that you do is meditate and release your intentions, your chances for success will be dubious at best.

The reason why is because most of us will experience resistance in the form of doubt. A sports car is a very distinct item, and it is expensive. Both the specificity of this intention, along with its cost, provides ample room for doubt to arise.

Conversely, if your intentions are to increase your income, that is an intention that is more general and can come from numerous sources. The intention to "increase your income" is more general than a sports car, and there are more avenues from which it can happen. For this reason, most people will find it an easier intention to manifest than a sports car.

With the intention of increased income, you have the opportunity to attract it through improving the way you handle your finances, getting a higher paying job, receiving an inheritance, starting your own business, and so on. All of these methods are recognized as available methods for increasing your income because that is how we have been socialized.

Because these methods are believable to us, they generate less resistance from us. On the other hand, trying to manifest a sports car directly, without effort on your part, seems less plausible to our minds; hence, the sports car is harder to manifest.

You may be wondering at this point as to the previous comment that having a more general intention makes it easier to manifest than having a detailed intention. After all, we frequently hear that our intentions should be made as real and concrete as possible. In other words, having a vivid image of the person that you want to attract into your life is more effective than having an intention that you want to meet someone. Which view is correct, making your intentions detailed and explicit, or making them general? The answer is that both views are right; it depends on your level of resistance.

Whatever you create in your life you must first create in your imagination.

– Tycho Photiou

Imagine that you want to manifest a new job and you make your intention as detailed as possible. As you meditate, you create a particular intention of the kind of job that you want. You know the salary you want, the people that you want to work with, and the distance of your commute. If you are not confident in your ability to manifest, you can quickly experience self-doubt as you wait for your manifestation to enter your life. You may start questioning your intention, wondering how realistic the idea of such a job presenting itself to you is. It is this questioning that will create resistance within you and prevent your dream job from manifesting. For this reason, you will probably be more successful if you are less detailed in your intentions and simply meditate on the intention that you want the job that will bring you happiness.

Until you become more confident in your manifesting abilities, it is better to make your intentions detailed for those things that do not have an emotional connection for you while making those intentions that have an emotional connection for you more general. As you gain confidence in your manifestation ability, you can become more detailed in all of your intentions.

From the perspective of higher levels of awareness, it is just as easy to manifest a multimillion-dollar mansion as it is to manifest a paper clip. It is only from our ordinary level of awareness that there appears to be a difference in difficulty when attempting to manifest these things.

Imagination is everything. It is the preview of life's coming attractions.

– Albert Einstein

Chapter 5: 30-Day Challenge

This 30-day challenge is offered to provide greater structure to the content that you have read so that you can apply it more effectively. Feel free to modify the 30 Day Challenge to your level of ability in manifesting.

Days 1-14

- Familiarize yourself with the exercises in Chapter 2 and choose those exercises that are relevant to you. If you are not familiar with the manifesting process, you may want to do all of them. If you have tried to manifest in the past but experienced obstacles, practice those exercises that you believe will address the areas that you need to develop further.

- Practice the exercises that you have selected for two weeks. This will allow you to gain confidence in your ability to perform them.
- It is recommended that you focus on no more than three exercises at a time. If you believe that you can benefit from doing additional exercises, take them on in Days 15-30.

Days 15-30

- Familiarize yourself with the exercises in Chapter 3 and choose the exercises that are relevant to you.
- Practice the exercises that you have selected for two weeks. This will allow you to gain confidence in your ability to perform them. Note: Due to its challenging nature, the exercise "Meditation on Self-Inquiry" should be done on an ongoing basis until you feel comfortable with it.
- It is recommended that you focus on no more than three exercises during this time. If you believe that you can benefit from doing additional exercises, perform these exercises after you complete Days 15-30. After completing Day 30, start the 30-Day Challenge over again by practicing these exercises on Days 1-14.

- If you still have exercises to practice from Chapter 2, perform these exercises during Days 15-30. After completing Day 30, start the 30-Day Challenge over again by practicing your selected exercises from Chapter 3 during days 1-14.
- Days 1-30: Refer to Chapter 4 as needed. Chapter 4 will provide you with guidance on how to deal with obstacles such as resistance and disempowering emotions.

This book is also available in audio format.

You can learn more at:

www.LOAforSuccess.com/audiobooks

Conclusion

We are approaching the end of this book now. Remember that the Law of Attraction is not an end unto itself. It is just a normal function of the universe and we can learn to use it consciously. However, the greatest things happen after diving deep and developing more awareness.

Upon achieving higher levels of awareness, it will become crystal clear to you that who we are is beyond our thoughts. As pure consciousness, we can manifest anything we want spontaneously without bigger effort. In order to get there, get committed to getting to know your true self and removing resistance. Schedule your LOA rituals time and enjoy the exercises from this book. We are all energy. Let's rise higher and enjoy the process! I am very curious to hear back to you.

If you have a few moments, please share your thoughts in the review section of this book and let us know which exercise you found most helpful. Your honest review would be much appreciated. It's you I am writing for and I would love to know your feedback.

Enjoy your LOA journey,

Elena

A Special Offer from Elena

Finally, I would like to invite you to join my private mailing list (my **VIP LOA Newsletter**). Whenever I release a new book, you will be able to get it at a discounted price (or sometimes even for free, but don't tell anyone 😊).

In the meantime, I will keep you entertained with a free copy of my exclusive LOA workbook that will be emailed to you when you sign up.

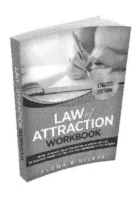

To join visit the link below now:

www.loaforsuccess.com/newsletter

After you have signed up, you will get a free instant access to this exclusive workbook (+ many other helpful resources that I will be sending you on a regular basis). I hope you will enjoy your free workbook.

If you have any questions, please email us at: support@loaforsuccess.com

More Books written by Elena G.Rivers

Available at: www.loaforsuccess.com

Ebook – Paperback – Audiobook Editions Available Now

Law of Attraction for Amazing Relationships

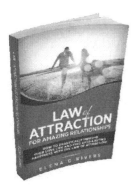

Law of Attraction for Weight Loss

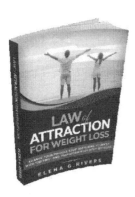

Law of Attraction for Abundance

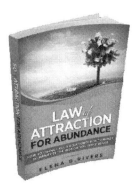

Law of Attraction to Make More Money

You will find more at:

www.loaforsuccess.com/books

Made in the USA
Middletown, DE
30 August 2021